AN
EGYPTIAN
CRAFTSMAN

Giovanni Caselli

PETER BEDRICK BOOKS
New York

Contents

Introduction

The people in this story lived in Egypt during the reign of the Pharaoh Rameses II. He ruled Egypt for 67 years from 1279 BC to 1212 BC.

They lived in a village known today as Deir el-Medina. It lay on the west bank of the River Nile, opposite the great city of Thebes and near to the Valley of the Kings, where the dead Pharaohs were buried. All the men in the village were employed by the Pharaohs to make splendid tombs for them. There were architects, stonemasons, sculptors, artists, bricklayers, laborers and scribes.

The village was originally built on the orders of Pharaoh Thutmose I, who died in 1493 BC. His name is stamped in some of the mud bricks. Over the next five centuries, the village grew and prospered, and by the time of Rameses II it had reached its greatest size. About 70 houses stood within its walls, with a further 40 or 50 outside. There was common land for the village animals and a communal well.

In this story, a man called Imhotep becomes a scribe. Scribes were very important civil servants. They were in charge of building supplies, of keeping lists of the work that had been done and of paying the workmen. The workmen were not paid in money but in flour, to make bread, and barley, to make beer. They were well paid, with enough to feed themselves and their families and some left over to exchange for other goods. Fish, vegetables, clothes, pottery, and even their houses, were all supplied. Occasionally there were bonuses of salt, oil and ox-meat. Scribes were very well paid, and some of them could afford farm land and slaves and were even able to build tombs for themselves.

At the end of this book, you can see some detailed pictures of the tools and equipment that Imhotep and his family might have used in their daily lives. There are also suggestions for places to visit and books to read.

Good News?

Kaha stood by himself in the middle of the village square. He didn't feel like playing with his friends today. Everyone else felt in a holiday mood. Soon it would be the festival of Opet, which lasted for three whole weeks. The men of the village would be home before long from their work on the Pharaoh's tombs to join in the feasting and processions.

Kaha's best friend, Hapu, got up from where he was sitting and came over to him.

'What is it, Kaha? You look very gloomy today.'

'It's my father,' Kaha replied. 'He's been promoted. He's going to become a scribe when the festival holidays are over.'

'But that's good news, surely!' said Hapu, surprised. 'Isn't it a great honor? Aren't you proud of him?'

'Well, yes, of course I am. It's good for him, and a great honor for our family,' admitted Kaha. 'But what about me?' He frowned and went on.

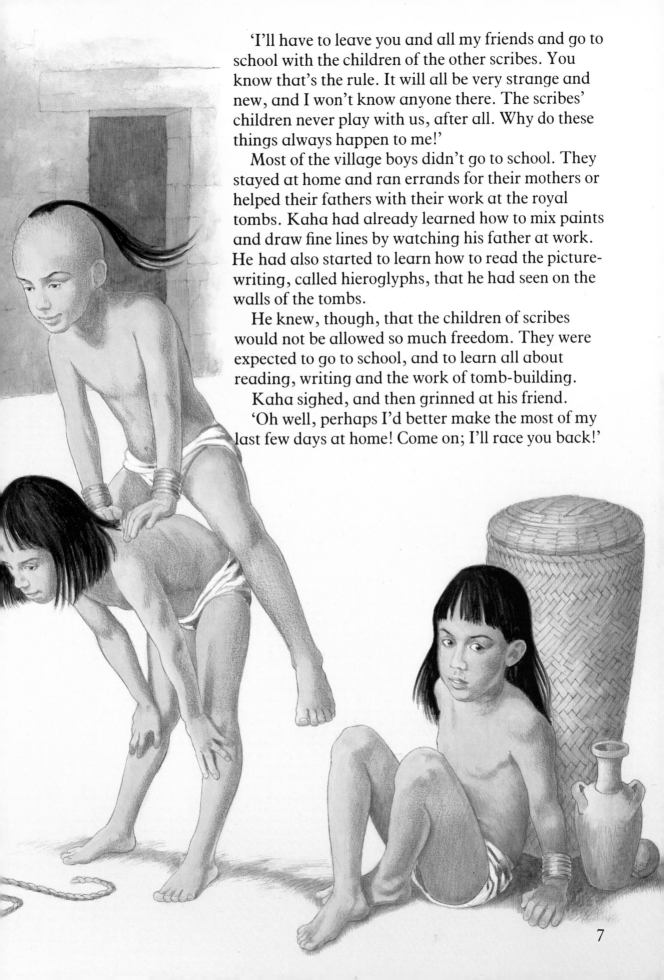

'I'll have to leave you and all my friends and go to school with the children of the other scribes. You know that's the rule. It will all be very strange and new, and I won't know anyone there. The scribes' children never play with us, after all. Why do these things always happen to me!'

Most of the village boys didn't go to school. They stayed at home and ran errands for their mothers or helped their fathers with their work at the royal tombs. Kaha had already learned how to mix paints and draw fine lines by watching his father at work. He had also started to learn how to read the picture-writing, called hieroglyphs, that he had seen on the walls of the tombs.

He knew, though, that the children of scribes would not be allowed so much freedom. They were expected to go to school, and to learn all about reading, writing and the work of tomb-building.

Kaha sighed, and then grinned at his friend.

'Oh well, perhaps I'd better make the most of my last few days at home! Come on; I'll race you back!'

At Work in the Tomb

It was dark inside the tomb, but Kaha's eyes had grown used to the flickering lamplight. He watched his father at work. Imhotep finished his drawing of the Pharaoh with a flourish. The pale, watery paint dried quickly on the newly-plastered wall. He went over the whole figure again using a thicker black paint, making a few changes here and there. He was working more slowly than usual today, taking care to do his very best. It was his last day as a draftsman. He had been promoted and after the festival of Opet he would start work as a scribe.

'I'll be sorry to leave all this,' he said to Kaha. 'I've enjoyed working on these paintings. But it will be even better to be a scribe.'

Kaha looked around him. At the end of the passageway was the burial chamber where the Pharaoh's body would be laid to rest in a stone coffin. The tomb was nearly finished; the stonemasons and plasterers had completed their building work and moved on to other tombs, but Menna, Imhotep's assistant, was still busy. He hummed to himself as he made a grid pattern on the wall, using a string dipped in paint. When he snapped the string against the wall he made a neat series of squares which helped Imhotep to arrange his drawings and hieroglyphs.

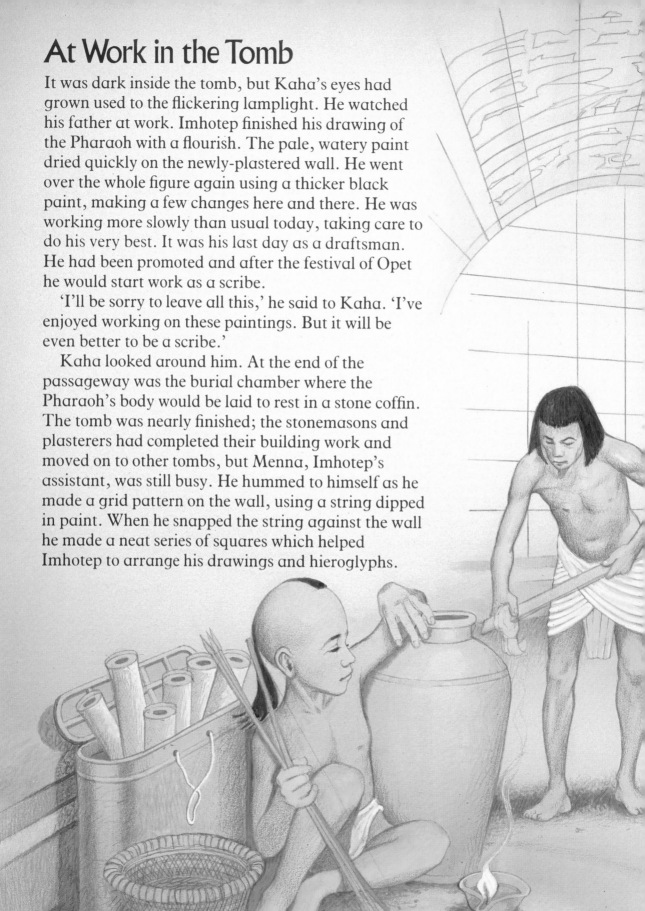

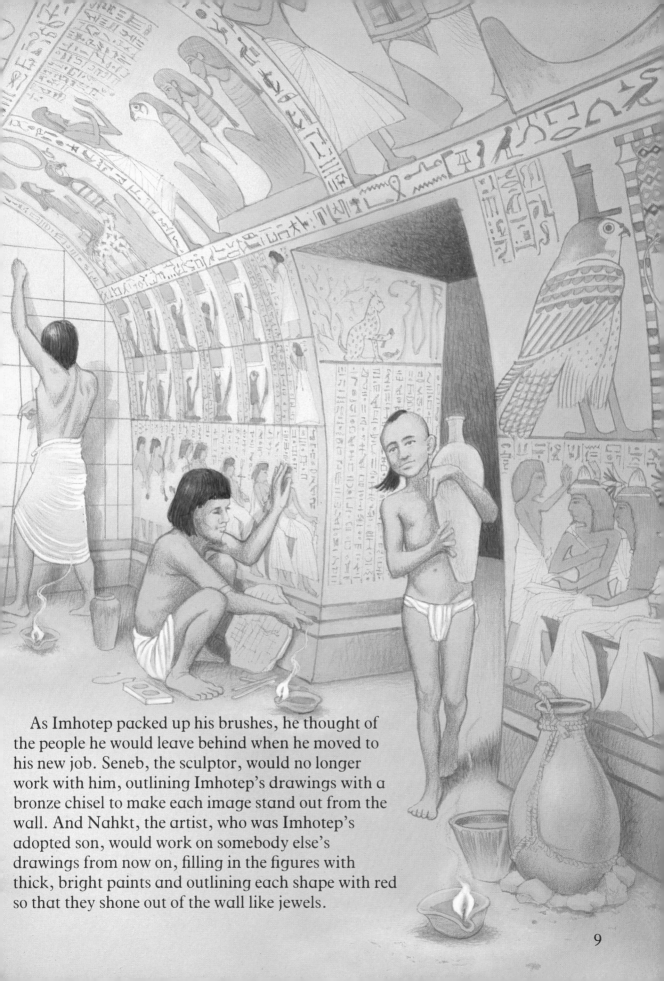

As Imhotep packed up his brushes, he thought of the people he would leave behind when he moved to his new job. Seneb, the sculptor, would no longer work with him, outlining Imhotep's drawings with a bronze chisel to make each image stand out from the wall. And Nahkt, the artist, who was Imhotep's adopted son, would work on somebody else's drawings from now on, filling in the figures with thick, bright paints and outlining each shape with red so that they shone out of the wall like jewels.

The Walk to the Village

Everyone chattered excitedly as they walked along the narrow, rocky path that led from the tombs to the village. They were glad to be going home. For eight days the craftsmen had worked deep inside the rock, sleeping in rough huts near the tomb entrance. Then they went home to the village for a three-day break, or sometimes for longer holidays at festival time. Suddenly Imhotep stopped. 'Look,' he cried, pointing to a hawk circling lazily overhead, 'there's the great god Horus!' They all gazed until the bird was out of sight, and then trudged on happily. Seeing the hawk had been a good omen. It meant that things would go well.

At last, they could see their village in the dusty valley below. They could just make out the narrow streets and whitewashed brick houses. Not far away, across the hills, the great River Nile flowed slowly through its flooded valley.

It was the season of Aket. Every year at this time the Nile burst its banks and flooded the surrounding countryside, covering the low-lying farmland. The festival of Opet was held at the height of the floods to celebrate the life-giving waters and the rich, black mud that was left when the waters went down. This mud became the fertile soil for next year's crops.

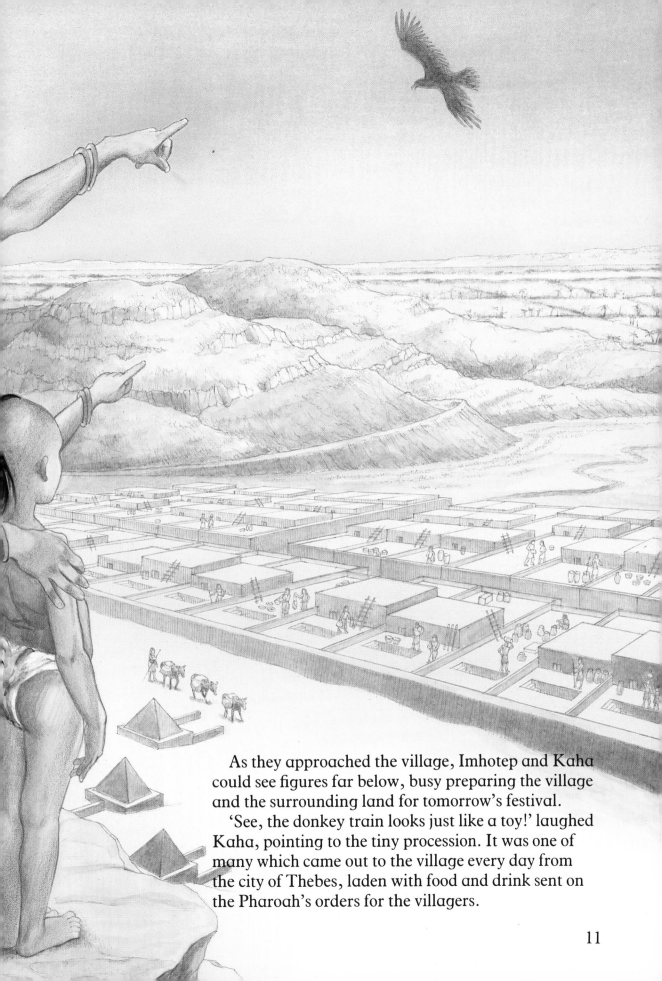

As they approached the village, Imhotep and Kaha could see figures far below, busy preparing the village and the surrounding land for tomorrow's festival.

'See, the donkey train looks just like a toy!' laughed Kaha, pointing to the tiny procession. It was one of many which came out to the village every day from the city of Thebes, laden with food and drink sent on the Pharoah's orders for the villagers.

Home at Last

Imhotep and Nahkt quickened their pace. Kaha found it hard to keep up with them. They were nearly home. They lived in the old part of the village, and as they hurried along the narrow streets, their shoulders brushed against the walls of the stone houses. Outside their door stood a large pitcher of water, filled every day from the village well. Nahkt stopped outside the house to splash his dusty face, but Imhotep hurried on. He rushed through the doorway decorated with red hieroglyphs which had been painted by his great grandfather. It was a long time since he had seen his wife and his other children.

'Hello, everyone! It's good to be back home again! What's that wonderful smell?'

Wia, his wife, laughed. 'All you ever think about is food,' she said, 'but supper won't be long!'

Nahkt and Kaha came through the doorway to join them. 'What's that wonderful smell? I'm starving!' asked Nahkt. Wia hugged him, and Kaha, too.

'You're as bad as your father! Now, go and wash properly, you two, and then come up to the roof and eat,' she said.

It was pleasant to sit out on the flat roof in the cool evening breeze. The servant brought them a meal of bread, radishes and a delicious lentil dish. There was beer to drink, too.

Suddenly, Imhotep exclaimed in pain, 'Ow! My tooth! More grit in the lentils! Or was it the bread?' Although the bread came all the way from the royal bakery at Thebes, no one could escape finding pieces of grit from the soft millstones in their bread or flour.

'Now,' said Wia, smiling, 'I've got some news. I've hired an extra servant to help me and the girls get everything ready for the festival.' She caught sight of Imhotep's frowning face and added quickly, 'Don't worry! It wasn't expensive. I exchanged a wickerwork basket I made for my share in the servant's time. I hear that she's a good cook!'

Imhotep laughed. Even Kaha forgot his worries about going to the new school as he listened to his older sisters, Makhajib and Ahuri, telling stories about the journey across the Nile to Thebes, where the festival was held, in earlier years. Taka, his youngest sister, soon fell asleep on Wia's lap, lulled by the family's voices. It was not long before the rest of the family joined her, settling down to sleep on the flat roof under the shining stars.

The Journey to Thebes

They made an early start while it was still cool. No one
wanted to miss the opening ceremonies of the festival!

It was a long walk from the tombmakers' village to
the ferry that would take them across the Nile to
Thebes. Ahuri chattered to her father as they walked.

'Do you think we'll meet Ipy?' she asked. Imhotep
was quite rich and owned some land outside the
village. This land was farmed for him by Ipy, an old
peasant, who grew fruit and vegetables on it and sold
them in the village.

14

'No, I don't think we'll meet him,' Imhotep
answered. 'He's probably moving the animals to
higher ground, beyond the reach of the flood.' He
hoped that they would not meet Ipy, who was usually
grumpy at this time of year. During the flood season,
when little work could be done on the land, the
peasants were forced to work on royal monuments
and other public buildings, by order of the
government. Ipy hated this and grumbled all the
time. But Imhotep was very fond of Ipy, and admired
his skill as a farmer. He smiled to himself as he
remembered the many friendly arguments they had
had about their favorite seasons.

'Peirt is best,' he would tell Ipy. 'Then there is
plenty of water to help the crops grow in the rich
black mud. There are fish and wild birds to hunt, too.
If you had to work in the Land of the Dead, as I do,
and see nothing growing all day long, then you'd
choose Peirt as your favorite season, too.'

Ipy would shake his head, and rub his gnarled old
fingers together. 'It's all right for you,' he'd say. 'But
I never stop work during Peirt. First there's seed to
be sown, then plowing the fields, building the
irrigation ditches, looking after the animals. No, give
me Shemu instead!

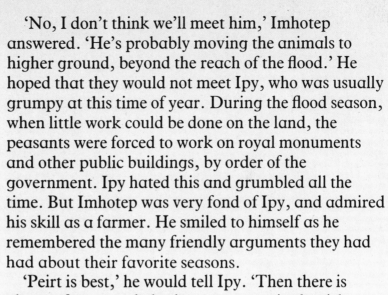

'In Shemu, the corn is ripe to be harvested and I
can catch up on the local gossip from all the people
who come to help gather the harvest. Once the
harvest's safely in, I can relax a bit, and watch the
donkeys threshing the corn and someone else
winnowing it and putting it into sacks. A full granary,
that's what I like to see!'

'Look, father, I can see buildings on the other side of
the river,' cried Kaha, suddenly. 'Is that really Thebes?'

The Festival of Ophet

By the time Imhotep and his family arrived in
Thebes, the normally busy streets were empty. All
the inhabitants had gathered on the banks of the
River Nile to wait for the arrival of the god Amun
from his temple at Karnak, in the north of Egypt.
The enticing smell of festival bread and beer wafted
from the temple kitchens. At the quayside, ships
unloaded all sorts of special foods and drinks for the
feasts that would be held after the god's procession
had passed through Thebes.

'Oh!' shouted Ahuri, 'I can see a beautiful little
house, all covered in gold!' Sure enough, shaven-
headed priests dressed in leopard skins were carrying
a miniature golden house towards the quay.

'There is a statue of Amun, the everlasting creator, inside,' Wia told her. More priests walked in a slow procession down to the river's edge, reading prayers from papyrus scrolls. On the temple canal, leading from the river, a gold-plated cedarwood barge bobbed gently at anchor. The priests placed the statue of the god on an altar in the middle of the deck.

'Look, look! There's the Pharaoh!' cried Nahkt. 'Can you see him, Kaha?' The Pharaoh went on board the barge with the priests and began to make prayers and offerings to Amun. There was a creaking sound and slowly the barge began to move through the water, pulled along by teams of strong men heaving on massive ropes.

Wia explained to Kaha that the barge would carry the statue of Amun to his temple at Luxor, not far away.

'You remember, don't you, that the god spends half the year here with us in the south and the rest of his time in his temple at Karnak? That is why we hold this festival now, to celebrate his arrival and the coming of the flood waters.'

17

In the Village Temple

Kaha woke up late. The family had not arrived home until the early hours of the morning. They left the festival at Thebes still in full swing, even though it was dark. They had to catch the last ferry.

'Oh, my feet are sore,' groaned Kaha, as he stretched them. He had walked miles yesterday. Nahkt had carried him the last part of the way home and the last thing he remembered was falling asleep across his brother's shoulders.

It had been very exciting in Thebes. Kaha remembered the taste of the warm bread and cool beer that his mother had bought from one of the hundreds of street-sellers. Best of all, he remembered the men from lands to the far south who had played the drums that made everyone want to dance. It was the first time Kaha had been to Thebes. He had been too young the year before.

Kaha got up. Today the family were going to the village temple. It was very different from the great temples at Karnak and Luxor. It was a small, simple building of rough stones held together with mud. Outside, it did not look all that different from Kaha's own home. But inside, you could tell it was a holy place. The soft light from the oil lamps fell on polished wood and white stone statues.

'Why are we going to the village temple?' he asked.

'Because I want to give thanks to the gods for my good fortune in becoming a scribe,' explained Imhotep. 'And for the gift of my family.' Imhotep had carved his prayers on small flat pieces of stone. Kaha and his sisters carried food to offer to the gods.

Inside the temple the priest was waiting. He was shaven-headed and dressed in a leopard skin like the priests at Thebes.

Imhotep and his children knelt before the statue of Hathor, the mother goddess.

'I remember your mother praying to Hathor for the gift of children when we got married,' said Imhotep. Kaha nodded. He had heard this before. The goddess had given Wia daughters at first. Then Wia and Imhotep had decided to adopt Nahkt so that Imhotep could pass on his craftsman's skills to the next generation. Then the gods had given them Kaha, who would also learn his father's skills.

Imhotep gave the food and the prayers to the priest who offered them to the goddess.

'The gods have been good to me so far,' said Imhotep. 'Let us pray that we will continue to find their favor.'

Preparations for the Feast

It was time to join in the preparations for their village's own festival. Wia checked that all was going well in the kitchen, and asked the slaves to bring plenty of water for washing. They all had a thorough wash, using a sticky paste soap and rinsing themselves in a large basin. When they had washed their hair, they poured on sweet-smelling oils and arranged it in curls and plaits, using combs made of wood and ivory. Imhotep and Nahkt shaved their arms and legs with hooked bronze razors. The servants helped them all to decorate the palms of their hands, the soles of their feet and their finger and toe nails with red henna. Kaha found it difficult to sit still while this was being done. It tickled dreadfully!

Wia loved dressing up for festivals. She sent the servant girl to find her cosmetics box, and started to put on her make-up.

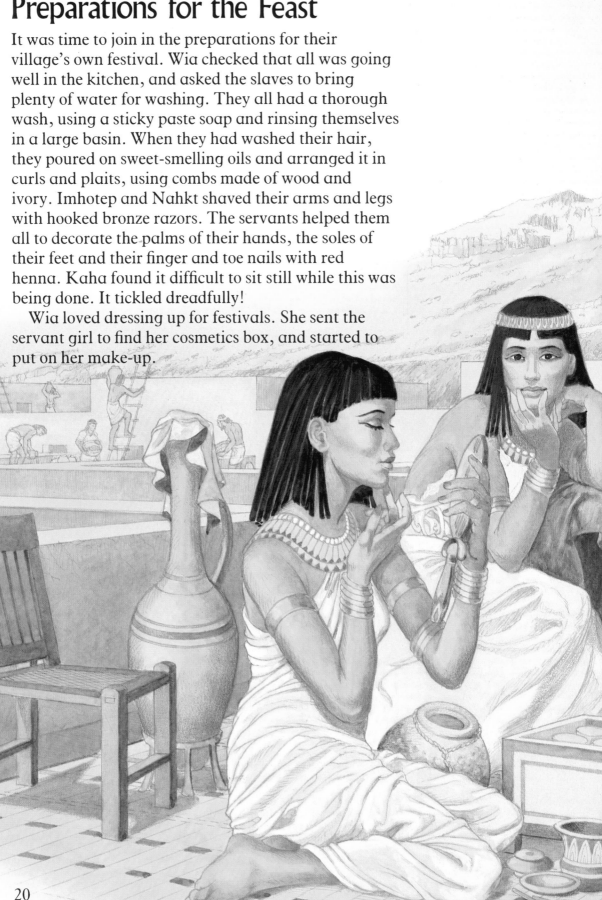

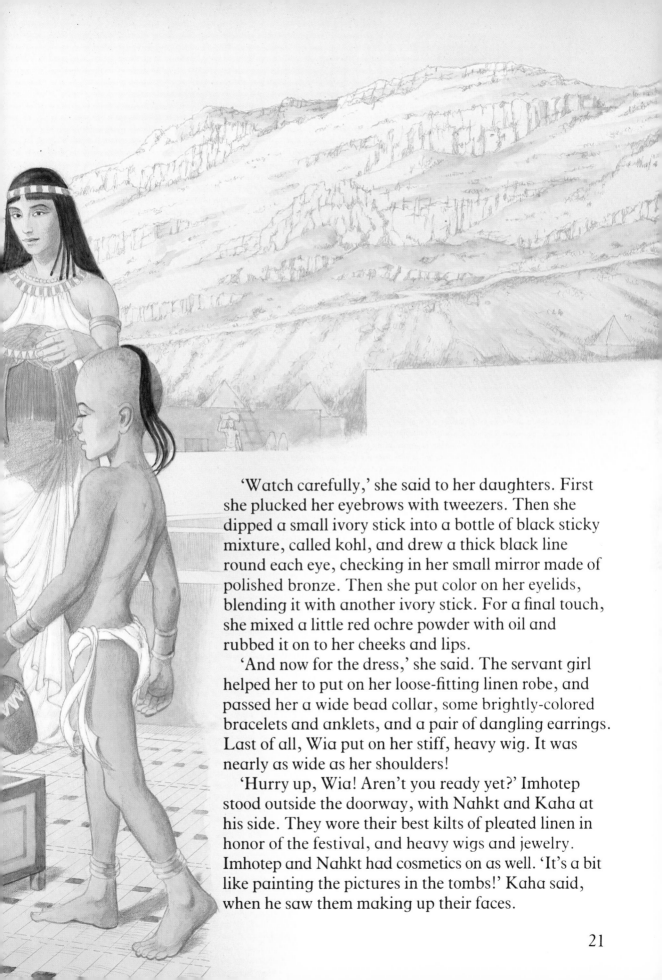

'Watch carefully,' she said to her daughters. First she plucked her eyebrows with tweezers. Then she dipped a small ivory stick into a bottle of black sticky mixture, called kohl, and drew a thick black line round each eye, checking in her small mirror made of polished bronze. Then she put color on her eyelids, blending it with another ivory stick. For a final touch, she mixed a little red ochre powder with oil and rubbed it on to her cheeks and lips.

'And now for the dress,' she said. The servant girl helped her to put on her loose-fitting linen robe, and passed her a wide bead collar, some brightly-colored bracelets and anklets, and a pair of dangling earrings. Last of all, Wia put on her stiff, heavy wig. It was nearly as wide as her shoulders!

'Hurry up, Wia! Aren't you ready yet?' Imhotep stood outside the doorway, with Nahkt and Kaha at his side. They wore their best kilts of pleated linen in honor of the festival, and heavy wigs and jewelry. Imhotep and Nahkt had cosmetics on as well. 'It's a bit like painting the pictures in the tombs!' Kaha said, when he saw them making up their faces.

Village Celebrations

The village feast was a great success. It had been very well organized. Chairs were arranged in groups under a shady linen canopy, which was decorated with garlands of flowers. Each family in the village had sent some of its best food for everyone to share, and some, like Wia, had hired extra servants to help.

'I can hardly hear the singing,' said Wia, 'we're all making too much noise! But look at that dancer over there! Isn't she good!'

The delicious smell of roast ox and ducklings cooked in honey floated across from where the servants were hard at work.

'I think Nahkt will eat the canopy if the food doesn't arrive soon!' laughed Imhotep. But the food did arrive, and they all started to eat eagerly.

22

Wia poured out red and white wines for her family
and neighbors. Everyone ate with their fingers.
Servants and helpers from the village walked between
the groups, offering extra food and wine.

'Ugh, my fingers are all sticky!' complained Wia.
But soon a serving girl brought jugs of water and
basins for them to wash their hands in.

The next course was lentils and chickpeas cooked
with herbs and spices, meat stew, fish, and a special
bread that had to be softened in water before it could
be eaten. There was plenty of fruit and vegetables to
follow. Lots of them had been grown by Ipy, on
Imhotep's land. Imhotep said that he could always tell
a lettuce from Ipy's vegetable patch just by smelling
it. Certainly, the lettuces, melons, grapes and
pomegranates were very good.

At last, even Nahkt had had enough to eat. All the
villagers sat in the evening sunshine, drinking wine,
telling stories and listening to the musicians. It was
not until long after the sun had set that Imhotep and
his family returned home to sleep. Everyone agreed
that it had been the best feast for years and years.

23

The Work of a Scribe

It was Imhotep's first day as a scribe. The festival was over and it was time to go back to work. He took Kaha with him, to show him what a scribe's work was like. Several other children crowded into the room to watch.

'Is it going to be very hard work?' asked Kaha.

'Well, it's a responsible job,' his father replied. 'I have to make sure that there are enough tools and materials to keep a gang working for a week or so. Then I have to arrange for all the worn-out or blunted chisels to be collected and sent to the village workshop to be recast. I have to order the wooden scaffolding and the leather buckets used to carry away builders' rubbish from the tombs, as well. And I have to make a daily record of all the work done at the tomb, and keep an account of how much oil is needed for the lamps, and how many lamp wicks are used each shift.'

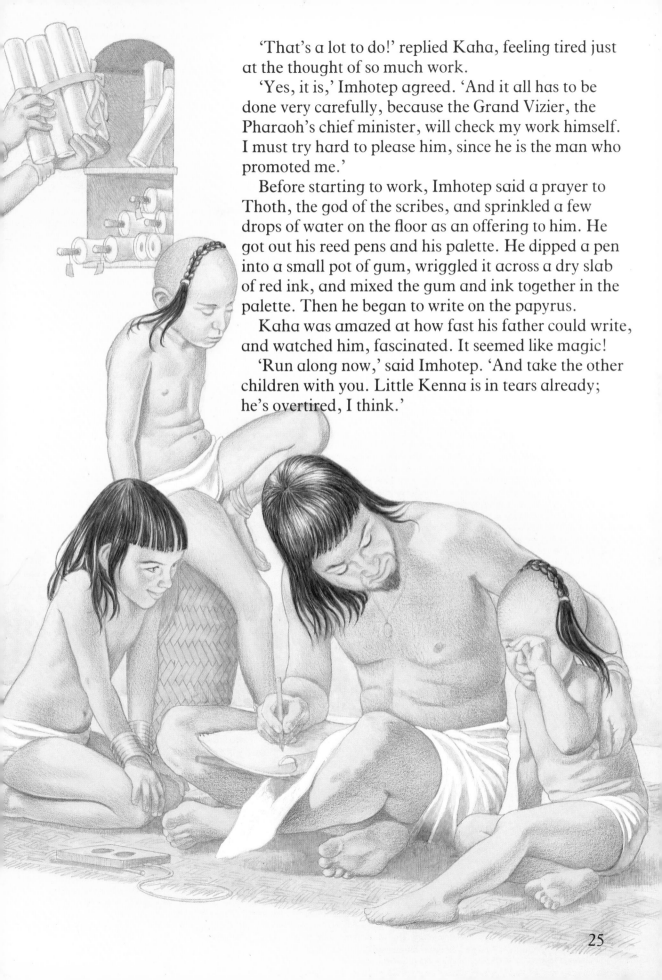

'That's a lot to do!' replied Kaha, feeling tired just at the thought of so much work.

'Yes, it is,' Imhotep agreed. 'And it all has to be done very carefully, because the Grand Vizier, the Pharaoh's chief minister, will check my work himself. I must try hard to please him, since he is the man who promoted me.'

Before starting to work, Imhotep said a prayer to Thoth, the god of the scribes, and sprinkled a few drops of water on the floor as an offering to him. He got out his reed pens and his palette. He dipped a pen into a small pot of gum, wriggled it across a dry slab of red ink, and mixed the gum and ink together in the palette. Then he began to write on the papyrus.

Kaha was amazed at how fast his father could write, and watched him, fascinated. It seemed like magic!

'Run along now,' said Imhotep. 'And take the other children with you. Little Kenna is in tears already; he's overtired, I think.'

First Day at School

Kaha was on his way to the scribes' school. Imhotep
had given him a set of new writing tools.

'Use them well, son,' his father had said. 'One day
you too will be a scribe. It is the greatest of all
professions.' And he had put on the white robe that
scribes wore and set off for his own new job. Wia and
her daughters looked on proudly: scribes were
respected and important members of the village
community. Then it was time for Nahkt to go to the
tomb, where he was taking over Imhotep's job as
draftsman, and for Kaha to go to school.

He walked along slowly and soon met some other
children on the way. At first he was a little shy, but he
soon plucked up courage to talk to one of the boys,
Ineni.

'What is it like at school? Is it hard?'

'Strict!' grinned Ineni. 'You get beaten if you make
any mistakes.'

'That's right,' added a taller boy. 'It's called the
"House of Life" but you wouldn't think so. It's so
dreary. We have to sit for hours without speaking.
And those stone benches are hard!'

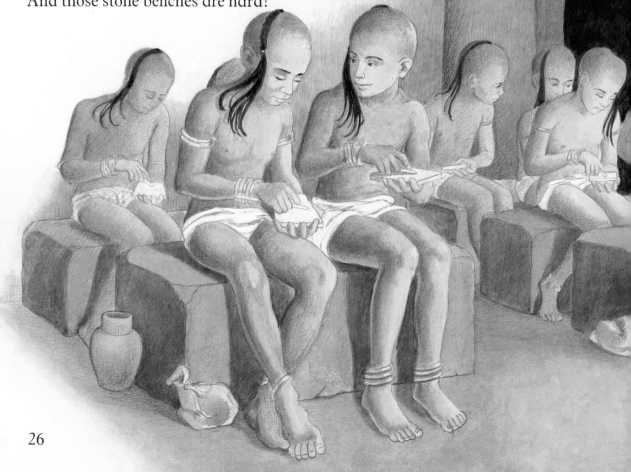

26

Kaha began to wish his father had never been promoted and that he could still be playing in the fields with his friends.

'Maybe they are just saying those things to frighten me,' he thought to himself.

School was every bit as hard as the children had described. Kaha had to learn the 700 picture signs of the Egyptian alphabet by heart. These were used on tombs and monuments. For everyday use and official documents there was a shorter version. And there were endless ancient prayers and sayings to memorize. But Kaha did not mind the hard work because he was learning to write. Very few people in Egypt had this skill, which was why scribes were so highly respected. At first it was difficult to hold his wooden palette in one hand, write with the other hand and balance his writing block on his knees at the same time. To begin with, the children practised on pieces of wood or stone that could be wiped clean. Kaha could hardly wait until his writing was good enough to use papyrus, the thick white paper made from the insides of the papyrus reeds that grew along the banks of the Nile. Then he would be on the way to being a real scribe, like his father.

Picture Glossary

Life under the pharaohs was concentrated along the River Nile.

The river is over 1000 km long but the fertile area each side of it, where everyone lived and farmed, was only 10 to 20 km wide. Along this fertile ribbon, the pharaohs built their great monuments and temples at the places named on the map (right).

The Egyptians firmly believed in life after death and thought of it as a continuation of their earthly life. That is why they had furniture, jewelry, personal treasures and food and drink with them when they died.

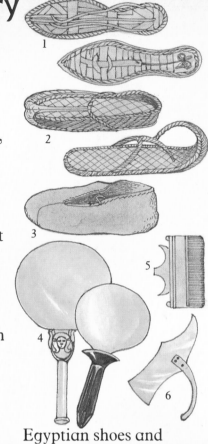

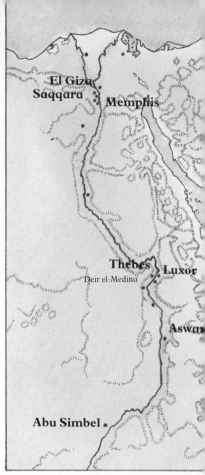

Egyptian shoes and personal belongings: sandals made of papyrus (1), and palm-leaf (2); leather shoe (3), bronze mirrors (4), a bone comb (5) and a bronze razor (6).

The inside of the great pyramid at El Giza, (below) showing the tomb chamber and secret passages. The mummified body of the pharaoh was laid in a wooden sarcophagus (below left).

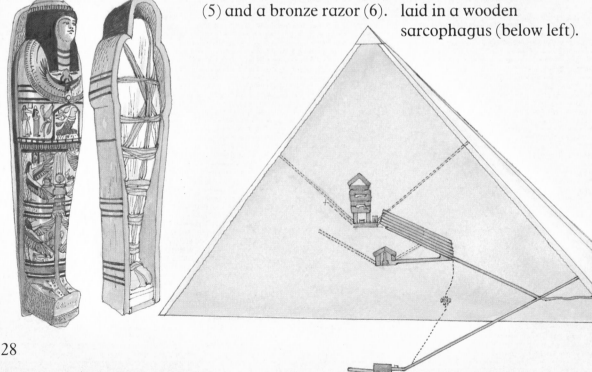

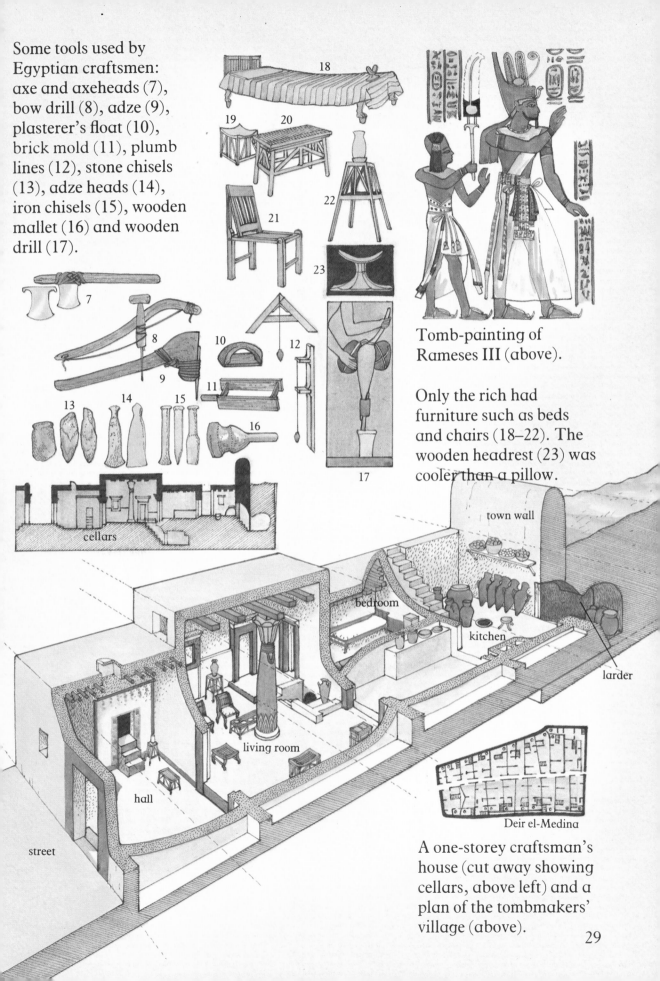

Some tools used by Egyptian craftsmen: axe and axeheads (7), bow drill (8), adze (9), plasterer's float (10), brick mold (11), plumb lines (12), stone chisels (13), adze heads (14), iron chisels (15), wooden mallet (16) and wooden drill (17).

Tomb-painting of Rameses III (above).

Only the rich had furniture such as beds and chairs (18–22). The wooden headrest (23) was cooler than a pillow.

cellars

town wall

bedroom

kitchen

larder

living room

hall

street

Deir el-Medina

A one-storey craftsman's house (cut away showing cellars, above left) and a plan of the tombmakers' village (above).

29

Finding Out More

Books to Read

The following books contain information about life
in Ancient Egypt, and about the wonderful buildings
and tombs built by Egyptian craftsmen:
J. Crosher **Ancient Cities** Macdonald Educational 1985
W. Boase **A Closer Look At Ancient Egypt** Archon
Press Ltd. 1977
P. Macaulay **Pyramid** Collins 1976
A. Millard **The Egyptians** Macdonald Educational 1975
G. Caselli **The First Civilizations** Peter Bedrick
Books 1985
J. Weeks **The Pyramids** Cambridge University Press 1976
P. Ventura and G.P. Ceserani **In Search of
Tutankhamun** Macdonald 1985

You will need an adult to help you read the following
books, but they contain a lot of fascinating
information:
J. Kamil **The Ancient Egyptians, How they Lived
and Worked** David and Charles 1976
T.G.H. James (editor) **An Introduction to Ancient
Egypt** British Museum Publications 1978